Countries
Fly Flags

and other questions about
people and places

Philip Steele

KINGFISHER
NEW YORK

KINGFISHER
LONDON & NEW YORK

Copyright © Macmillan Publishers International Ltd 2012
Published in the United States by Kingfisher,
175 Fifth Ave., New York, NY 10010
Kingfisher is an imprint of Macmillan Children's Books,
London.

First published 1995 by Kingfisher

Consultant: Keith Lye

Distributed in the U.S. and Canada by Macmillan, 175 Fifth
Ave., New York, NY 10010

Library of Congress Cataloging-in-Publication data has been
applied for.

ISBN: 978-0-7534-6793-0

Kingfisher books are available for special promotions and
premiums. For details contact: Special Markets Department,
Macmillan, 175 Fifth Ave., New York, NY 10010.

For more information, please visit www.kingfisherbooks.com

Printed in China

9 8 7 6

6TR/0318/UTD/WKT/128MA

Illustrations: Peter Dennis (Linda Rogers Associates); Chris
Forsey; Terry Gabbey (AFA); Luigi Galante (Virgil Pomfret
Agency); Maureen Hallahan (B.L. Kearley) lettering; Tony
Kenyon (B.L. Kearley) all cartoons; Angus McBride (Linden
Artists); Nicki Palin.

CONTENTS

What is a country?

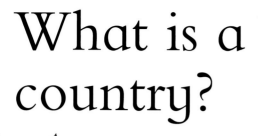

A country is an independent land with its own government. The government runs the country, and makes laws that the people must obey. A country has its own name, and its borders are normally agreed by other countries around the world.

Each country has its own money, called currency, with its own coins and banknotes. There are rubles in Russia and pesos in the Dominican Republic.

All countries have their own stamps, which often carry a picture of the country's ruler. Some stamps show a country's wildlife or mark an important discovery.

People wave their national flags at parades, sports events, and celebrations.

GERMANY

CHINA

GREECE

BRAZIL

SWEDEN

ISRAEL

Why do countries fly flags?

Every country has its own flag, which is a kind of national badge. Each country's flag is different. The design may include colored stripes, star and sun patterns, or religious signs such as crosses or crescents. Flags are flown on special occasions as a symbol of a country and its people.

Every country has its own special song called a national anthem. It is sung to show respect for a country and its history.

SOUTH AFRICA

AUSTRALIA

UNITED KINGDOM

CANADA

TURKEY

ARGENTINA

SOUTH KOREA

JAMAICA

AUSTRIA

Which country has the most people?

More than one billion people live in China, and more than 50,000 new babies are born there every day. You would think that meant a lot of birthdays, but in China everyone celebrates their birthday at the same time—the Chinese New Year!

Chinese New Year is celebrated by Chinese people all over the world in late January or early February. There are spectacular street processions.

HAPPY BIRTHDAY

One of the world's biggest-ever parties was on July 4, 1991. It celebrated the birthday not of a person but of two countries—the U.S. and Canada. More than 75,000 people turned up!

Which is the biggest country?

Russia is so big that it takes eight days to cross it by train! As children set off for school in the city of Moscow in the west, others are already going home in the eastern port of Vladivostok.

MOSCOW

VLADIVOSTOK

Where is there land, but no countries?

The vast frozen land around the South Pole is called Antarctica. It is not a country—it has no people, no government, and no flag. Many countries have signed an agreement promising to keep Antarctica as a wilderness for scientists to study.

No one lives in Antarctica except for a few hundred scientists, who go there to study rocks, the weather, and plant and animal life.

How many countries are there?

There are more than 190 independent countries in the world, but the exact number changes from year to year. This is because new countries are sometimes made. East Timor was the first new country of the 2000s, in 2002, but others have been made since then.

1 Guatemala
2 Belize
3 El Salvador
4 Honduras
5 Nicaragua
6 Costa Rica
7 Panama
8 Cuba
9 The Bahamas
10 Jamaica
11 Haiti
12 Dominican Republic
13 Antigua & Barbuda
14 Dominica
15 Barbados
16 St. Vincent & the Grenadines
17 Trinidad & Tobago
18 Ecuador
19 Ireland
20 United Kingdom
21 Belgium
22 Netherlands
23 Luxembourg

24 Switzerland
25 Liechtenstein
26 San Marino
27 Vatican City
28 Italy
29 Monaco
30 Andorra
31 Denmark
32 Estonia
33 Latvia
34 Lithuania
35 Czech Republic
36 Austria
37 Slovakia
38 Hungary
39 Slovenia
40 Croatia
41 Bosnia & Herzegovina
42 Serbia
43 Montenegro
44 Kosovo
45 Macedonia
46 Albania
47 Greece

48 Bulgaria
49 Moldova
50 Malta
51 Cyprus
52 Lebanon
53 Israel
54 Jordan
55 Armenia
56 Azerbaijan
57 Kuwait
58 Bahrain
59 Qatar

Some small Pacific island countries are not shown on this map: Fiji Islands, Kiribati, Marshall Islands, Federated States of Micronesia, Nauru, Palau, Tonga, Tuvalu, and Samoa.

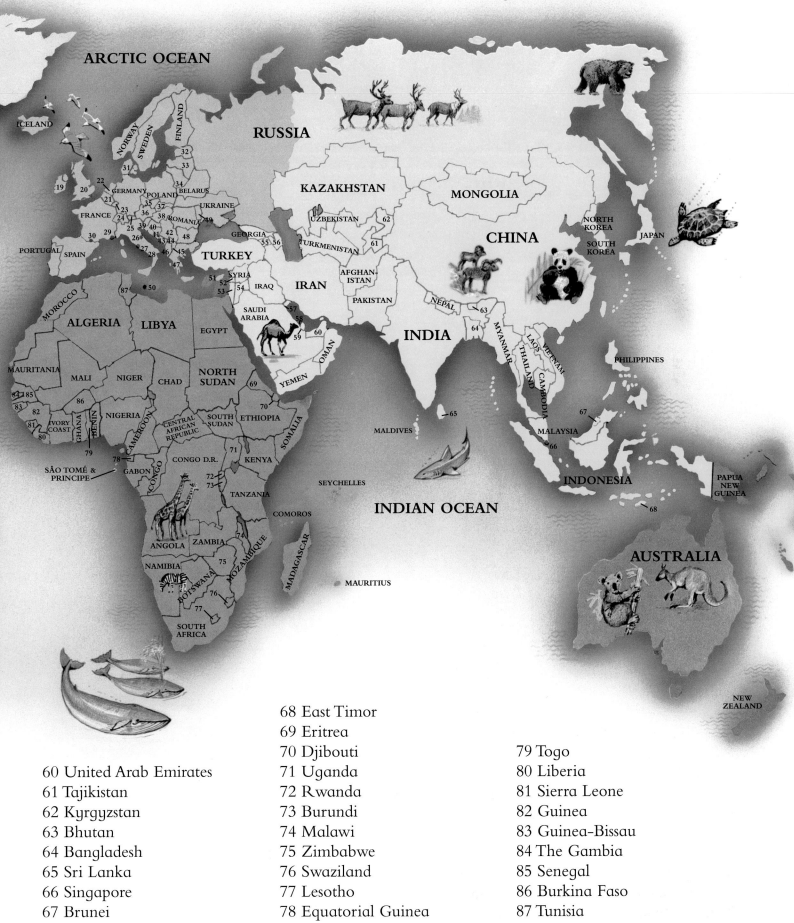

60 United Arab Emirates
61 Tajikistan
62 Kyrgyzstan
63 Bhutan
64 Bangladesh
65 Sri Lanka
66 Singapore
67 Brunei
68 East Timor
69 Eritrea
70 Djibouti
71 Uganda
72 Rwanda
73 Burundi
74 Malawi
75 Zimbabwe
76 Swaziland
77 Lesotho
78 Equatorial Guinea
79 Togo
80 Liberia
81 Sierra Leone
82 Guinea
83 Guinea-Bissau
84 The Gambia
85 Senegal
86 Burkina Faso
87 Tunisia

9

Which city is above the clouds?

The city of Lhasa is in Tibet, a part of China. It is built close to the edge of the Himalayas, the world's highest mountains. Lhasa is so high that it's often covered by clouds, which blanket the city in a thick, wet mist!

Some people call Tibet the "Roof of the World," because it is so high up in the mountains.

You have to climb 1,000 steps to reach the Potala Palace, which towers above the streets of Lhasa. It's very grand—even its roofs are made of gold!

Why do Venetians walk on water?

The Italian city of Venice is built on dozens of tiny islands in a sheltered lagoon near the sea. In between the islands are canals, which form the main "streets" of the city. To get from one part of Venice to another, you don't take a bus or a train—you catch a motorboat or a gondola.

A country's capital city is where the government works. Washington, D.C. is the capital of the United States. The president lives there, in the White House.

Which is the world's biggest city?

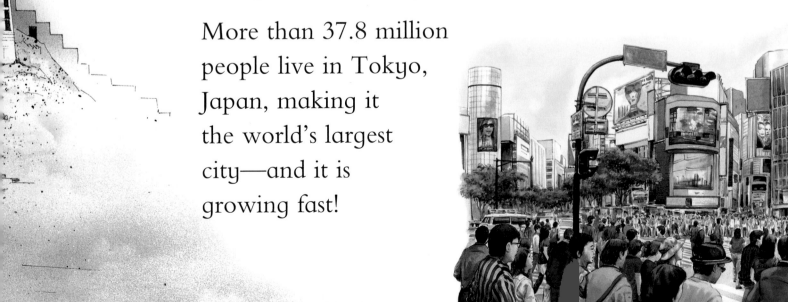

More than 37.8 million people live in Tokyo, Japan, making it the world's largest city—and it is growing fast!

Who writes with a paintbrush?

The art of beautiful handwriting is called calligraphy. Japanese children learn calligraphy at school.

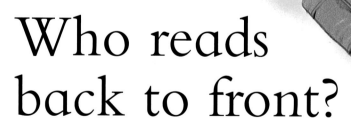

In China and Japan handwriting can be an art. Instead of dashing something off with a pen, people sometimes paint words slowly and beautifully with a brush and ink. Artists often frame their work, and hang it on the wall like a picture.

About 50,000 different symbols may be used to write Chinese. Luckily, school children only have to learn about 5,000 of them.

Who reads back to front?

To read a book in Arabic or Hebrew, you have to work from right to left. So if this book was in Arabic, the first page would be where the index is now.

Which country has more than 800 languages?

Papua New Guinea is a land of many languages. Most of the people live in small villages, deep in the rainforest, or high up in the misty mountains. Some are so cut off from one another that their languages are very different.

In many areas of Papua New Guinea, people can only talk to each other through a translator.

Around 5,000 languages are spoken around the world. Here are just a few ways to say "hello."

Jambo!

Namaste!

¡Hola!

Cześć!

Dag!

Swahili   **Hindi**   **Spanish**   **Polish**   **Dutch**

There's a place in New Zealand with 85 letters in its name. And there's another in France with only one!

Y

Taumatwhakatangihangakoauaotamateaturipukakapikimaungahoronukupokaiwhenuakitanatahu

Who lives in a longhouse?

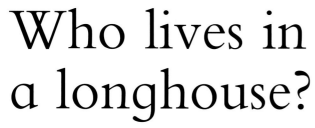

As many as 100 families may share the same longhouse.

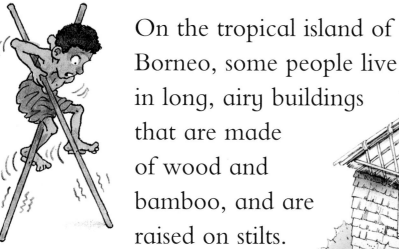

On the tropical island of Borneo, some people live in long, airy buildings that are made of wood and bamboo, and are raised on stilts. These longhouses are home to dozens of different families, each with their own room.

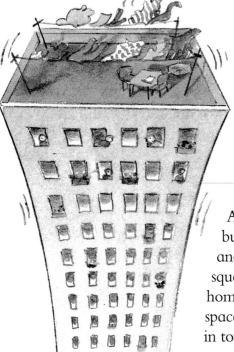

Apartment buildings are another way of squeezing a lot of homes into a small space. You find them in towns and cities.

Where do gardens grow on rivers?

In the Netherlands, many people live on barges moored on the country's canals. Boat owners don't have gardens, of course, but some of them grow flowers on the roof!

How do you stay cozy in the Gobi?

The Gobi Desert is in Mongolia in northern Asia and its winters are icy cold. Some shepherds and their families travel around the desert, living in thick felt tents called yurts, which keep out the hot sun or the freezing cold.

Which is the oldest dish on the menu?

Pancakes may be the oldest dish of all. Even Stone Age people baked them! The basic recipe—milk, eggs, and flour—is the same all over the world, but the kind of flour changes from place to place. Pancakes can be made using flour from potatoes, maize, wheat, or oats.

All over the world, people pound grains such as maize to make flour for their pancakes.

In different parts of the world you might find almost anything on your plate—from crunchy insects or chewy snails to snakes, guinea pigs, or even sheep's eyes!

Who eats shells, butterflies, and little worms?

Table manners change from place to place. The British think you're rude if you put your elbows on the table while the French think it's perfectly fine!

We do! These are all types of pasta—their Italian names are conchiglie (shells), farfalle (butterflies), and vermicelli (little worms). Pasta is a dough made from flour and water, which is cut into shapes and cooked. It's delicious simply served with a tasty sauce and a sprinkling of cheese.

Vermicelli

Farfalle

Conchiglie

Pasta dough comes in more than 100 shapes and sizes including stars, snail shapes, and all the letters of the alphabet.

Where does it take all afternoon to have a cup of tea?

In Japan there's a special ancient tea ceremony called chanoyu. The tea is made so slowly, and sipped so carefully, that it truly does take hours. It's not a good idea to turn up to the ceremony feeling thirsty!

Where do women wear derby hats?

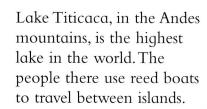

In the Andes mountains of South America, many of the women wear round derby hats. The hat has become a part of their traditional dress, along with full skirts and brilliantly colored llama-wool shawls and ponchos.

Derby hats were first made for men, not women! British businessmen wore them to work for more than 100 years.

Where do men wear skirts?

On special occasions in the Highlands of Scotland, it's traditional for men to wear kilts. These pleated skirts are made of a checked woolen cloth called tartan. Kilts are warm, but they come down only to the knee, so they are worn with a pair of long, woolen socks.

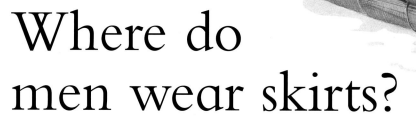

Which dress has no stitches?

The Indian sari is a simple length of cloth that wraps neatly around a woman's body. It has no stitching, buttons, or zips, and its design hasn't changed very much for hundreds of years. Saris are made of bright cottons or shimmering silks, and on a hot day they are delightfully cool and comfortable to wear.

People who live in desert countries traditionally wear long robes and head cloths to protect them from the heat and dust. In Arctic countries people wrap up warmly in fur-lined anoraks and parkas.

In Scotland, each family group has its own tartan, with a particular pattern and color.

Who wears banknotes at their wedding?

At a Greek or Turkish wedding, the guests don't take the bride and groom gifts—they give them money instead. At the wedding party, guests pin banknotes all over the couple's clothes. Often there is so much money that it completely covers their clothes!

On the island of Madagascar, a man makes a speech to his bride-to-be before she will marry him. If the speech is no good, he pays a fine and starts again!

Hindu brides decorate their skin with beautiful, lacy patterns for their wedding day. They use a reddish-brown dye called henna.

Where are children made kings and queens?

On January 6, French families enjoy a special dinner together. At the end of the meal, the children eat slices of a flat almond pie called a galette. In one of the slices a charm is hidden, and whoever finds it is crowned king or queen for the night.

Who sticks out their tongue at strangers?

One of the customs of the Maori people of New Zealand is to stick out their tongues, pull faces, and make loud noises to scare strangers who come to their village (or *marae)* before accepting them as friends.

Where do children watch shadows?

Javanese puppets are made of painted leather. The puppeteer moves them with wires or rods.

Shadow puppet shows are enjoyed by people all over the world. On the Indonesian island of Java, the audience sits on both sides of a cloth screen. One side watches the puppets, while the other sees the shadows dance, as if by magic!

In a Vietnamese water puppet show, the story is acted out on the surface of a lake. It can't be much fun for the puppeteers—they have to stand in the water.

22

Who makes pictures from sand?

The Navajo people of the southwestern United States create beautiful pictures with grains of colored sand. The pictures are made on the ground for special ceremonies. But these works of art don't last for long—they are destroyed afterward!

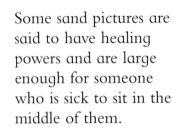

Some sand pictures are said to have healing powers and are large enough for someone who is sick to sit in the middle of them.

In Switzerland, cow herders used to play alpenhorns— long wooden horns that echoed from one mountain to another.

Which dancers snap their fingers?

Flamenco dancing comes from southern Spain. Proud-looking dancers toss their heads and snap their fingers, as they stamp and whirl to the music of a Spanish guitar.

Where are wheat fields bigger than countries?

The rolling grasslands of Canada and the U.S. are planted with wheat as far as the eye can see. One Canadian wheat field was so big, it was double the size of the European country San Marino!

Huge combine harvesters have to work in teams to harvest the gigantic wheat fields.

More people eat rice than wheat. Rice plants need to stand in water, and are grown on flooded land called paddy fields.

Where does chocolate grow on trees?

Chocolate is made from the seeds of the cacao tree. Sadly, the trees don't grow everywhere—only in the hot, wet parts of South America, southeast Asia, and west Africa.

Which country has more sheep than people?

In Thailand, coconut farmers train monkeys to harvest their crop. The monkeys scamper up the trunks of the palm trees and throw down the fruit.

Although there are about 23 million people in Australia, most live around the coast. In the center, people run enormous sheep farms. At the last count, there were over 74 million sheep—about three times the number of people!

Who rides on a snowmobile?

A dog team can pull a sled about 50 miles (80km) in a day. A snowmobile covers that in an hour.

Many of the people who live in icy Alaska and northern Canada travel across the frozen snow on powerful sleds called snowmobiles. Not long ago, sleds were pulled by huskies, but nowadays these are only raced for fun.

Trains in Tokyo, Japan, are so crowded that railroad staff called crushers have to push in the passengers while the doors close.

Fishermen in Portugal paint "magic" eyes on their boats to watch over them at sea and bring them safely to harbor.

Where do you park your bike in China?

There are millions and millions of people in China, and millions and millions of bikes! So all Chinese cities have huge cycle parks, where an attendant gives your bike a number, and helps you find it again later.

Who paints pictures on trucks?

The truck drivers of Afghanistan are very proud of their trucks. They paint holy pictures all over them, covering every last inch in bright, colorful patterns. Even the lug nuts are painted different colors.

The Afghans may drape their trucks with silver chains, and even stick on pull-tabs from soda cans as decorations.

Why do people race camels?

Dromedaries can race at over 12 mi. (20km) an hour—faster than two-humped camels.

One-humped camels are so sturdy and fast that in hot desert areas they are ridden like racehorses. The races are very popular in Saudi Arabia, and large crowds cheer the camels as they speed across desert racetracks.

People have been known to race all types and sizes of animals—from ostriches to snails!

The world's fastest ball game is called pelota. The ball is hurled from a wicker scoop at the speed of an express train.

Which is the world's most popular sport?

Soccer balls are kicked about in more than 160 countries around the world. The game is played by millions of people—in playgrounds, parks, streets, and, of course, soccer fields.

The earliest soccerlike game was called zuqiu. It was played 2,400 years ago in ancient China.

Where do elephants glow in the dark?

For the Sri Lankan festival of the Esala Perahera, elephants are decorated with beautiful hangings and strings of electric lights. More than 50 elephants take part in a nighttime procession, along with thousands of drummers and dancers, who crack whips and wave colorful banners.

The leprechaun of Irish folktales is a little green man. The green shamrock is Ireland's national plant.

When do people eat green food?

Saint Patrick is the patron saint of Ireland, and green is the country's national color. Saint Patrick's Day falls on March 17, and for Irish people everywhere it's a time of wild celebration. Some people even dye party food and drinks green!

When is the Day of the Dead?

The Day of the Dead is a Mexican holiday that takes place every year on November 2—All Souls' Day. People remember dead friends and relatives by taking flowers and candles to their graves, and having picnics there.

Brightly painted papier-mâché skeletons are made for the Day of the Dead celebrations.

February is carnival time in many countries, with glittering parades and music.

The Esala Perahera procession takes place in Kandy, Sri Lanka, at the time of the July full moon.

Index